EXPLORING MILITARY CAREERS

JOBS IN THE U.S. COAST GUARD

JESSIE GEORGE

NEW YORK

Published in 2023 by The Rosen Publishing Group, Inc.
29 East 21st Street, New York, NY 10010

Portions of this work were originally authored by Judy Silverstein Gray and Taylor Baldwin Kiland and published as *Careers in the U.S. Coast Guard*. All new material in this edition was authored by Jessie George.

Cataloging-in-Publication Data

Names: George, Jessie.
Title: Jobs in the U.S. Coast Guard / Jessie George.
Description: New York : Rosen Publishing, 2023. | Series: Exploring military careers | Includes glossary and index.
Identifiers: ISBN 9781499469950 (pbk.) | ISBN 9781499469967 (library bound) | ISBN 9781499469974 (ebook)
Subjects: LCSH: United States. Coast Guard--Juvenile literature. | United States. Coast Guard--Vocational guidance--Juvenile literature.
Classification: LCC VG53.G464 2023 | DDC 363.28'60973--dc23

Some of the images in this book illustrate individuals who are models. The depictions do not imply actual situations or events.

Manufactured in the United States of America

CPSIA Compliance Information: Batch #CSRYA23. For further information, contact Rosen Publishing, New York, New York, at 1-800-237-9932.

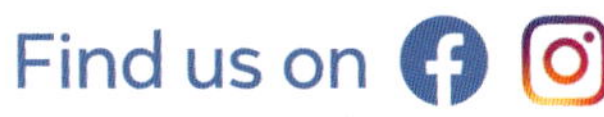

CONTENTS

CHAPTER 1

CENTURIES OF SERVICE

Though it has not always had the same name, the United States Coast Guard has a centuries-long history of protecting the nation's ports. Its earliest missions in the young days of the United States were mainly related to regulating commercial interests, but the service has evolved to be a flexible force for maritime protection across the globe.

ANTIPIRACY POLICIES

The United States faced a growing national debt after the American Revolution, and the young country had trouble generating income to pay it. Alexander Hamilton, the first secretary of the treasury, came up with a plan to place taxes on imported goods brought into U.S. ports by foreign ships. The plan made sense, but piracy on the high seas and unpredictable weather were major threats to merchants who sought the safety of American ports. Life at sea was often hazardous.

As the first secretary of the treasury, Alexander Hamilton came up with policies for generating revenue and protecting merchant ships.

Hamilton was born and raised on the island of Nevis in the Caribbean, so he was familiar with smuggling ships that avoided paying taxes. He was well aware that piracy interfered with trade and national security.

In 1787, Hamilton was focused on coming up with a plan to create a maritime service with flexible capabilities. In an essay from *The Federalist Papers*, he argued that the United States should invest in a small fleet of well-armed ships that could stand guard at

U.S. ports to protect merchants and citizens both. To create an organization that could fulfill this new patrol task, Hamilton established America's Revenue Cutter Service. A cutter is a ship that is 65 feet (19.8 m) in length or longer. By founding the service, Hamilton ensured that his new tax collection plan would be able to succeed, helping generate funds for the young United States. The Tariff Act of August 4, 1790, included the purchase of a fleet of ten cutters. For this reason, Hamilton is often considered the father of the Coast Guard. As part of this new cutter fleet, he also provided 100 people to collect tariffs on

The Revenue Cutter Service was the first form of what would eventually become the U.S. Coast Guard.

the goods that could now safely come into American port towns. These supporters also kept an eye out for threats to the security of these ports, kicking off a U.S. tradition of service to the nation—with an emphasis on maritime safety and security.

Because it was closely tied to collecting taxes, this new force was sometimes called the Revenue Marine. Overall, it operated as a maritime police force protecting U.S. coasts. Each of the new cutters had a crew of 10 sailors, each of whom earned a modest monthly salary. Hamilton also asked Congress to give each of these sailors a military rank.

These crews were made up of experienced sailing men who were also well-educated in the nation's laws. One of their primary tasks was to conduct inspections of documents such as ship cargo lists, called manifests. They were often required to seize vessels that were violating the law. The important missions given to those first Revenue Cutter sailors required ships that were both fast enough to chase larger vessels at sea and quick enough to navigate safely through shallow ports and busy harbors. Ships were often given names appropriate for these tasks, such as *Diligence* and *Vigilant*, because they were always standing watch. Other vessels were named after American Revolution heroes such as Adjutant General Alexander Scammell. Still others were named for the 13 original states, including the *Massachusetts*. Many of the original vessel names that were assigned to ships in the early days of the

Revenue Cutter Service are still used by the Coast Guard on newer vessels.

The first officer to receive a commission in the Revenue Cutter Service was Hopley Yeaton of New Hampshire. Yeaton made a name for himself by serving in the Continental Navy during the Revolutionary War. President George Washington appointed him to the outdated rank of "master of a cutter" in the Revenue Cutter Service on March 21, 1791. He was assigned to the 57-foot (17.4 m) schooner *Scammel*.

KEEPING THE LIGHT

The Coast Guard has been involved in safeguarding life and property at sea since the 1700s. Around the time of the American Revolution, there were very few buildings along shorelines, and much of the new nation's coast was rocky. Night passage by ships could be dangerous, especially in windy or stormy weather. The early American colonies first constructed lighthouses in 1716 to help provide safer passage for ships by lighting the way to shore. These old lighthouses used lanterns lit by candles or whale oil, and they were staffed by brave volunteers. By 1812, lighthouse keepers were specifically assigned to lighthouses by the government, and they often used whale oil to ensure that their lanterns could burn continuously through the night. After 1822, some lighthouses were equipped with a special lens that could magnify or bend the light, thus providing better illumination for ships crossing over rocky channels.

In addition to keeping lanterns aflame, lighthouse keepers also had to rally volunteers to help rescue mariners at sea. Tales of courageous lighthouse keepers are an important part of the Coast Guard's rich search-and-rescue legacy. Today, some of the Coast Guard's cutters bear the names of early lighthouse keepers. Many women served dutifully in these roles, as did war veterans. The United States Lighthouse Service, officially formed in 1910, became part of the Coast Guard in 1939.

Though it officially existed for less than three decades, the U.S. Lighthouse Service's legacy lives on in the modern Coast Guard.

EARLY U.S. WARS

Although captains of ships in the Revenue Cutter Service received official military ranks, they were not initially seen in open battle. It was not until 1798 that the service proved its battle readiness during the Quasi-War with France. This conflict's unique name came from the fact that neither side officially declared war and battles were almost entirely at sea.

The conflict erupted after the French seized U.S. ships as a protest of the new trade market emerging between the United States and Britain. To respond to this action, the young U.S. Congress authorized President John Adams to acquire and arm up to 12 vessels. All treaties with France, a former ally, were canceled. During the Quasi-War, the Revenue Cutter Service saw the vessel *Pickering* successfully capture 10 ships. The ship-based service did its job well, and the war ended in 1800 when French aggression declined and a treaty was signed.

In the early 1800s, the new United States found itself at war with Great Britain for a second time. Just as in the Quasi-War, vessels flying the flag of the United States were being harassed overseas. This time, it was British vessels disrupting American merchants and shippers. In what became known as the War of 1812, the U.S. Navy asked for assistance from the Revenue Cutter Service because the sleek ships of the service could more easily navigate in ports of shallower water. This war was the first of soon to be many "brown water wars," a name referring to conflicts that are fought closer to shore.

On the night of June 12, 1813, the Revenue Cutter vessel *Surveyor*, with its crew of 16 sailors, was captured by the British frigate HMS *Narcissus* after hand-to-hand combat in the Chesapeake Bay. By this point in the War of 1812, the courage and expertise of Revenue Cutter crews had become legendary. Though the *Surveyor* was captured, the service achieved many other successes in the conflict.

The early Coast Guard saw action as it supported the U.S. Navy during the War of 1812.

The Revenue Cutter Service became the first official U.S. military service to capture a British ship when the *Vigilant* captured the British ship HMS *Dart* on October 4, 1813.

SAVING LIVES, FIGHTING WARS

In 1832, the secretary of the treasury ordered the Revenue Cutter Service to assist mariners in the dangerously cold winter months. By 1837, lifesaving had become one of the key missions of the service.

This was the foundation of work performed by modern-day Coast Guard crews.

At a time when sailors were using simple instruments and the stars to navigate the world's waters, a life at sea was often dangerous. To help protect sailors, volunteer lifesaving forces were created in the United States. In Massachusetts, lifesaving stations were ready to deploy life jackets, life cars (gear and pulley systems), and sometimes even horse-drawn carts and small lifesaving boats. By 1848, numerous such stations could be found along the Atlantic and Pacific coasts, the Gulf of Mexico, and the Great Lakes to assist mariners. By 1854, full-time station keepers were paid by the government.

In 1871, Sumner Kimball became chief of the Treasury Department's Revenue Marine Division. Kimball convinced Congress to provide a budget of $200,000 to outfit and staff lifesaving stations. The secretary of the treasury was also allowed to employ full-time crews, and in 1878, a network of lifesaving stations were officially organized into the Life-Saving Service.

On January 28, 1915, President Woodrow Wilson signed the Act to Create the Coast Guard, combining the Life-Saving Service and the Revenue Cutter Service to finally establish the modern-day Coast Guard. By the time the act was signed, a network of more than 270 stations was already providing service in areas near the Atlantic Ocean, the Pacific Ocean, coasts along the Gulf of Mexico, and the Great Lakes. With the government's new push to formalize the Coast Guard, this important service could now be better provided to mariners and commercial shippers.

However, the Revenue Cutter fleet was still a substantial military force. Even after the conclusion of the War of 1812, the United States was only able to enjoy a brief time of peace. From 1836 to 1839, the service was called upon to help fight the Seminole Indian Wars on Florida's inland rivers and waterways. This series of conflicts arose after Seminole Native Americans started attacking U.S. settlers who moved onto their former lands.

During the Seminole Indian Wars, the Coast Guard's fleet provided invaluable support to the U.S. Marine Corps by supplying shallow-draft vessels that could blockade the coasts and help with amphibious landings. These ships also contributed to the success of shore battles during the Mexican-American War (fought between 1846 and 1848), which was fought over a land dispute in what is now the state of Texas.

SERVICE IN THE 19TH CENTURY

In the early 19th century, the Revenue Cutter Service was also called on to intercept ships that were participating in the slave trade. Though the practice was outlawed in 1808, Africans were still often chained in the lower decks of ships coming to the United States. Slavery was one of the most hotly debated topics in the mid-1800s, and the election of Abraham Lincoln to the presidency led to the Civil War. This

IDA LEWIS: SAVING LIVES

Credited with saving at least 18 lives, Idawalley Zorada Lewis—along with her mother—were in charge of the Lime Rock Lighthouse in Newport, Rhode Island. The two took over for Ida's father after he suffered a stroke in 1857. At the time, Ida was not even 15 years old. She served until her death on October 24, 1911. President Ulysses S. Grant personally paid Ida a visit after word of her frequent and heroic rescues eventually made it all the way to the White House. In 1924, more than 50 years after Ida began her service, Lime Rock Lighthouse was renamed Ida Lewis Lime Rock Lighthouse. This marked the first and only time that a lighthouse was named for a keeper. In 1995, the Coast Guard also named a buoy tender stationed at Newport in her honor.

Ida Lewis was one of the first American women to serve in the Coast Guard with distinction.

conflict saw brothers battling brothers as Southern states—which had seceded to form the Confederate States of America—fought to prevent the abolition of slavery. The Civil War would go on to become the deadliest conflict in U.S. history, but after it was done, slavery came to an end in the country.

The Revenue Cutter Service's vessel *Harriet Lane* fired the first shots of the Civil War on April 11, 1861, in South Carolina. There were few maritime Civil War battles, but when the service was called upon, its sailors performed their jobs with honor. Following President Lincoln's assassination in 1865, Revenue Cutter personnel were also tasked with searching ships for assassins.

A few decades after the end of the Civil War, it appeared that conflict was just over the horizon—again. Tensions began to rise between the United States and Spain in the late 19th century, and the closest Spanish holding was the island of Cuba. After the USS *Maine*, a peacekeeping vessel, exploded in Cuba's Havana Harbor, peace was no longer an option. Though it was later determined that the Spanish were not responsible for the *Maine*'s destruction, the Spanish-American War had already broken out. During this nearby international conflict, the Revenue Cutter Service expanded its protective duties beyond America's coastline. The service's primary mission was joining its navy counterparts in 1898 to form a blockade around Havana Harbor. During the war, the Revenue Cutter Service also staffed lifesaving stations and helped them double as observation posts, providing a critical and useful line of homeland defense.

When President Wilson formally established the U.S. Coast Guard in 1915, he named Captain Ellsworth Price Bertholf as its first commandant.

The heroic and effective Ellsworth Bertholf helped shape the modern Coast Guard.

Bertholf was an excellent candidate to lead the Coast Guard in its expanded missions to protect lives at sea. As part of the Overland Expedition of 1897–1898, his crew successfully rescued a fleet of nearly 300 whaling ships that were trapped by ice near Point Barrow, Alaska. Creativity, flexibility, adaptability, and physical stamina—all considered good characteristics for those serving in the Coast Guard—were the defining characteristics of Bertholf's service. He later led a similar and challenging rescue-and-relief mission in Russia. Bertholf and his team were awarded the Congressional Medal of Honor for their courageous efforts rescuing mariners.

In 1895, Bertholf became the first Revenue Cutter officer to join the Naval War College in Newport, Rhode Island. He had also proudly led the Revenue Cutter Service and supervised the development of an ice patrol after the *Titanic* sank because of an iceberg. Starting in 1911, Bertholf served as commandant of the Revenue Cutter Service, navigating the relatively underpowered branch through political storms that continually threatened to shut down its existence.

As the first commandant of the Coast Guard, Bertholf wanted to execute his vision for what this service could achieve. He wanted the new branch to be busy, taking on dangerous missions and protecting lives all over the globe. His courageous spirit lives on in today's Coast Guard, which prides itself on being a capable livesaving service that also has the potential for deployment as a maritime military force.

CHAPTER 2

UPDATES TO THE GUARD

The first century of the United States was defined by its many conflicts. However, as the young nation protected its independence, it grew stronger. The Coast Guard grew along with it, and by the 20th century, the United States was ready to compete with the rest of the world with its economic and military strength.

THE EARLY 20TH CENTURY COAST GUARD

The Coast Guard saw its earliest 20th-century action after the United States entered World War I. Though Americans were hesitant to join in a European war after so many conflicts in the 1800s, Germany's actions against the nation eventually took peace off the table. In April 1917, five American merchant ships were destroyed by German submarines off the American coast. In response to this attack, President Wilson asked Congress to declare war on Germany and its allies. It was viewed as the only way to protect the global interests of the U.S. and its allies. In World War I, as during previous wars, the Coast Guard was operated under the authority of the navy. To protect the security of U.S. ports, the Coast Guard was given missions to seize enemy merchant ships in U.S. harbors. These actions quickly restored control of domestic waterways, which otherwise may have been vulnerable. Six Coast Guard cutters—the *Tampa*, *Seneca*, *Yamacraw*, *Ossipee*, *Algonquin*, and *Manning*—also sailed overseas to Gibraltar. There, these vessels joined with the Atlantic fleet, earning high praise for their work protecting ships. However, after successfully escorting more than 350 vessels, the cutter *Tampa* was unexpectedly struck by a torpedo and sunk. It was a tragic loss and the largest single seagoing loss of American life during World War I. Crews assigned to the *Tampa*, *Seneca*, and *Ossipee* protected more than 1,500 merchant ships as part of

Though the United States did not want to enter World War I, President Wilson was forced to act to protect the nation.

nearly 300 convoys. The *Seneca* was also responsible for the rescue of 139 survivors from four ships that had been torpedoed.

After World War I, Coast Guard crews patrolled coasts around the United States and Alaska. These patrols were tasked with performing search-and-rescue missions, though it had less than 5,000 members. In 1919, after the Eighteenth Amendment was passed to outlaw the manufacture, sale, and transportation of alcohol, Coast Guard missions were adapted to include enforcement of smuggling laws. In 1922, the service rescued 3,000 mariners, but rumrunners—smugglers who illegally transported rum and other alcoholic beverages—posed a tricky challenge that had to be addressed.

As with its search-and-rescue missions, the Coast Guard often found itself understaffed to successfully complete its law enforcement tasks and protect U.S. ports. Despite the longtime staffing shortage, Coast Guard crews in 1927 captured the treacherous Horace Alderman. This smuggler, known as the Gulf Stream Pirate, had evaded the law for years, but he was finally captured 35 miles (56.3 km) off the coast of Florida. While several Coast Guardsmen were transporting a Secret Service agent to the small island of Bimini, Alderman attacked. A violent gun battle left two Coast Guardsmen and one FBI agent dead. Alderman was hanged for murder on the high seas in August 1929 at Coast Guard Base Six near Fort Lauderdale. A dangerous criminal, confirmed smuggler, and murderer, Alderman is the only person ever hanged by the Coast Guard.

FLYING THROUGH WORLD WAR II

During the decades of the 1920s and 1930s, the Coast Guard rapidly expanded its aviation program. The service's airpower grew from a single borrowed seaplane in 1920 to 50 aircraft, 7 air stations, and 2 air detachments by 1938. Daily air patrols of Gloucester Harbor, Massachusetts, helped slow down rumrunners. The additional development of amphibious aircraft, capable of taking off and landing on water, helped the Coast Guard rescue mariners in distress.

After World War I, airpower became a major concern for the United States, and the Coast Guard added airplanes to its arsenal.

In 1935, as the shadow of war was again emerging in Europe, the United States passed the Neutrality Act. This new policy was intended to provide aid to U.S. allies and prevent arms and ammunition from reaching the hands of the nation's enemies. As part of its enforcement of the Neutrality Act, the Coast Guard seized more than 60 German and Japanese ships in U.S. ports. As the name of this act implies, however, the United States was not eager to join in yet another war. It hoped that actions on the home front would help keep the country neutral.

Hopes for peace died when Japanese planes launched a surprise attack on the American fleet in Pearl Harbor, Hawaii, on December 7, 1941. The Coast Guard ships *Taney*, *Kukui*, *Reliance*, *Walnut*, and *Tiger* were part of the immediate military response. As an attack force of Japanese fighter jets flew overhead, American crews courageously fired back to prevent further destruction. After the Japanese withdrew, the Coast Guard was called on to secure the entrance to Honolulu Harbor.

After the Pearl Harbor attack, the United States officially entered World War II. As in previous conflicts, the Coast Guard again found itself transferred and now operated under the power of the Department of the Navy. Coast Guard crews boarded the Norwegian fishing vessel *Buskoe*, in Greenland, and discovered radio equipment. The crew revealed that it had intended to establish a station for Germany.

In 1942, early in the war, Douglas Munro—a 22-year-old Coast Guard signalman from Washington

BREAKING THE ICE

Especially in the early days of the United States, it was extremely important that merchants and goods could freely flow to and from the nation's ports. To protect the country's economy, the Coast Guard has long been asked to clear shipping lanes to allow imported and exported goods, such as fuel and oil, safe passage through ports. From clearing light harbor ice in eastern seaports to full-size icebergs in Alaska, the Coast Guard's icebreaking missions keep international commerce moving. The early cutters *Bear*, *Corwin*, and *Thetis* were specifically built to withstand ice and help rescue whalers and fishermen. However, the Coast Guard's first true icebreakers were built in 1926. Today, the Coast Guard supervises all icebreaking duties for the U.S. military. Modern icebreaker vessels are capable of barreling through hundreds of miles of thick ice at a time.

Icebreaker ships have unique designs that allow them to safely plow through ocean ice.

State—took control of a wooden Higgins boat to assist with an amphibious Marine Corps rescue mission. As he navigated his boat between enemy fire and troops, Munro worked tirelessly to provide enough cover for the marines. Returning one last time to ensure a full and safe rescue, Munro was shot and he eventually died. He is the Coast Guard's first and only recipient of the Medal of Honor for his extremely heroic actions during this operation. The modern Coast Guard cutter *Munro* is named for this brave soldier.

The Coast Guard performed many critical missions as part of World War II. More than 800 cutters and nearly 200,000 sailors conducted convoy escorts. Coast Guardsmen specifically played a key role. The Coast Guard made it possible to get troops ashore during the D-Day invasion at Normandy, France. The Battle of Normandy, one of the most famous battles of the war, was one of the most important steps in helping the United States and its allies achieve victory over Germany. The Coast Guard also provided expert sailing expertise for troops battling in the Pacific, played a significant part in most major World War II amphibious landings, and harnessed its sailors' boat-handling talents and skill during many search-and-rescue missions.

On February 23, 1945, Bob Resnick faithfully stood deck watch off the Japanese island of Iwo Jima. This small island had been the scene of fierce fighting. After U.S. marines successfully gained a foothold on Iwo Jima, Resnick supplied an American flag and

The Coast Guard played a major part in the famous raising of the U.S. flag at Iwo Jima.

a long pipe for use as a flagpole to the marines. As they struggled to hoist it above the volcanic sands that carpet the top of Mount Suribachi, American photographer Joe Rosenthal captured the moment in an image for the Associated Press. This sight became one of the most iconic symbols of the U.S. military during World War II. The hoisting of the flag after days of deadly combat on foreign soil is immortalized at the Marine Corps War Memorial in Arlington, Virginia.

Domestically, on the eastern seaboard of the United States, the cutters *Bedloe* and *Jackson* patrolled the coast of North Carolina. These vessels were on the hunt for German U-boats, or submarines. While trying to rescue a damaged ship, both the *Bedloe* and *Jackson* were sunk in the Great Atlantic Hurricane of 1944. In all, there were fewer than 20 survivors from these Coast Guard vessels. It is these important sacrifices in a relatively small military service that made a difference in the security of the nation's waterways.

During the war, the Coast Guard maintained lighthouses and other navigational aids, cleared important sea channels of dangerous ice, and ensured that enemy spies were not able to enter through U.S. ports. Using dogs and horses, the Beach Patrol kept a lookout on 95,000 miles (152,887 km) of the U.S.'s potentially vulnerable coastline, protecting residents from enemies. Coast Guard Captains of the Port also ensured that merchant and military cargo was safely transported. They helped establish the groundwork for port, cargo, container, and marine safety. These expanded duties prompted the Coast Guard to not only found a women's reserve (called SPARs) but also rely on the national draft to fill personnel shortages. It was during this time, as well, that Black Americans were formally integrated into the Coast Guard service.

NEW ACTION IN ASIA

When North Korean forces invaded South Korea in June 1950, the United States reacted quickly to ally itself with the democratic nation of South Korea. Fortunately, some Coast Guard officers had been informed about the invasion. Their units were stationed at a former Japanese naval base in South Korea, training members of what would eventually become the South Korean navy. During the Korean War, more than 20 cutters served at remote weather stations in the Pacific Ocean, gathering data about approaching storms for military aircraft.

Special outposts, called long-range aid to navigation stations, dotted across the Pacific Ocean allowed Coast Guard crews to share important information with other armed service branches. In January 1953, the Coast Guard performed a search-and-rescue role when units learned that Chinese forces shot down a reconnaissance plane in the U.S. Navy.

As the U.S. Marine Corps and U.S. Army saw heavy action on the front lines of the Korean War, the Coast Guard served mainly as it typically had.

Its primary mission was to defend ports and ensure their safety. Cutter crews were responsible for verifying identification from merchant ships that were still operating during the war. The Coast Guard also monitored shipments of dangerous military equipment, including weapons and ammunition. As the conflict in Korea stretched on, the Coast Guard grew to include more than 30,000 members. This increase in new sailors helped broaden the service's peacetime responsibilities while allowing it to maintain flexibility during times of war.

CHAPTER 3

THE COAST GUARD IN THE COLD WAR

Immediately following World War II, the Soviet Union and the United States entered into a time of high tensions called the Cold War. Though the two nations never directly fought, there was a global power struggle between the Soviet communist economic system and the American capitalist society. Vietnam became a battlefield for this power struggle in 1954, after Vietnamese communist revolutionaries successfully fought off the French, who had colonized the country. The new Vietnamese rulers split the country in two, making two states: North and South Vietnam. Over time, communism threatened to spread from North to South, prompting the United States to get involved to support the democratic south.

NAVIGATING VIETNAM

During the Vietnam War, the Coast Guard's experience in handling small boats, especially in shallow-water ports, proved its value. The service was called upon to support a new coastal surveillance force that was developed in 1965 to conduct riverine operations. As U.S. military leaders realized that the North Vietnamese Vietcong were using the nation's rivers and small waterways to ship large quantities of arms, supplies, and soldiers, shallow-water expertise was in high demand. Coast Guard boats helped detect enemy activity as nearly 60,000 vessels called junks and sampans crossed Vietnam's 1,200-mile (1,931 km) coastline. U.S. efforts to intercept North

Vietnam is a nation of many rivers and waterways, which made the Coast Guard a natural choice to support the U.S. military during the Vietnam War.

Vietnamese vessels that were smuggling weapons led to Operation Market Time. This mission would include the Coast Guard's 82-foot (25 m) small boats that featured in-shore maneuverability and effective weapons. The Department of Defense deployed the Coast Guard in Vietnam to act similarly to how the service operated domestically. The strategy paid off, as the Coast Guard's experience with surveillance and coastal defense improved the overall effectiveness of U.S. naval forces.

During the first month of Operation Market Time, Division 11 boarded more than 1,000 sampans, inspected more than 4,000 small boats, and established blockades that improved security for troops from South Vietnam and the United States. Coast Guard boats also provided medical evacuation, gunfire support, and transport for Special Forces troops. The Coast Guard was effective in capturing enemy weapons and supplies, disrupting their operations, and diminishing their capabilities. The service provided constant support for more combat-oriented U.S. naval forces. Working with the navy, the Coast Guard provided protection all along the South Vietnam coastline, reducing the effectiveness of enemy resupplies.

PROTECTING THE SEAS

During the decades after the Vietnam War, the United States began to pass additional environmental protection laws. In support of this goal,

Coast Guard missions were expanded to include enforcing environmental conservation laws, protecting commercial fisheries, and responding to marine disasters. These new operations created a skilled workforce that helped ensure the safety and health of the coastal zone. With duties ranging from patrols to documenting the health of fish species to oil-spill prevention and cleanup, Coast Guard marine science technicians supervised pollution response. Coast Guard personnel also inspected cargo and containers to ensure that environmental and safety laws were followed. Coast Guard staff boarded ships to inspect cargo, checked containers arriving in U.S. ports, and tested water samples. Their work was performed with cooperation from Coast Guard crews that monitor navigational signs, keep waterways running smoothly, and perform search-and-rescue missions.

As protectors of the coast, Coast Guardsmen and women help maintain healthy oceans, rivers, and fishery stocks. Sometimes, the Coast Guard is required to enforce fishing regulations by boarding ships to measure catches and to educate crew members about fishing bans and changes in local or national laws.

U.S. maritime services have been conducting conservation operations for two centuries, dating back to 1822. In that year, Congress ordered the Revenue Cutter Service to help prevent the cutting of live oak trees in Florida. Crews navigated through winding, narrow inland waterways to protect these vulnerable hardwood trees.

In addition to its lifesaving missions, the Coast Guard has long been involved in environmental protection operations.

In 1973, the International Convention for the Prevention of Pollution by Ships set some of the earliest standards for oceans across the globe. The Coast Guard's marine environmental protection duties are important to preserving healthy oceans and waterways.

On March 24, 1989, the vessel *Exxon Valdez* ran aground, spilling more than 11 million gallons (42,000,000 L) of oil into Prince William Sound in Alaska. The Coast Guard helped assist and direct a lengthy cleanup effort along more than 350 miles (563 km) of coastline. Cleaning up this manmade disaster took more than 450 boats and the coordination of many federal, state, and local agencies over many years. Skimmers, barges, cutters, and aircraft were used to help in the massive environmental cleanup operation. This damaging spill and the necessary cleanup mission led Congress to pass the Oil Pollution Act in 1990. This new law allowed the Coast Guard to enforce more strict regulations on oil tankers and their owners and operators. After the spill, the Coast Guard developed tighter controls on vessel traffic to further protect the marine environment.

The Coast Guard assists in cleanup efforts and wildlife preservation after manmade ecological disasters like oil spills.

As part of its response to pollution incidents, the Coast Guard generally coordinates the actions and aid of federal agencies. At the *Exxon Valdez* spill, for example, the Coast Guard was in charge of supervising the massive cleanup operation on the shoreline. It involved the hand-cleaning of marine mammals, shorebirds, and vessels. The long and expensive operation relied on longstanding partnerships with other agencies, such as the National Oceanic and Atmospheric Administration (NOAA), the Environmental Protection Agency (EPA), and the Department of Defense. Civilian groups, state agencies, and Exxon itself also participated in the cleanup operation.

Coast Guard inspectors undergo extensive training on how to properly investigate a ship's cargo, how to educate commercial mariners and marine industries about proper container storage, and how to prevent oil spills and pollution incidents. Even with these prevention strategies, pollution incidents still occur. For that reason, the Coast Guard staffs a National Response Center, where pollution incidents, including oil or chemical spills, and other maritime security incidents can be reported.

On April 20, 2010, another spill of historic proportions occurred when a deepwater oil drilling rig stationed off the coast of Mobile, Alabama, exploded. Tragically, 11 people were killed in the incident, which also sent oil spewing into the Gulf of Mexico. Nearly three months later, the oil well's head was finally capped. By then, 200 million gallons

(757,000,000 L) of oil had been introduced into local waters. The spill had a dramatic impact on more than 16,000 miles (25,749 km) of coastline in several states. The pollution affected many species of fish and marine animals, as well as shorebirds. This incident—the largest oil spill in U.S. history—was also the largest activation of Coast Guard reservists since the September 11, 2001, attacks.

NO TIME OFF

Coast Guard crews train constantly to improve their skills, even during times of peace. Working in the maritime environment can be dangerous. For example, the 180-foot (55 m) buoy tender *Blackthorn*—based in Galveston, Texas—had just completed a major shipyard overhaul in the port of Tampa, Florida, when it headed out to return home. Around 8:00 p.m. on January 28, 1980, the *Blackthorn* collided with the 605-foot (184 m) oil tanker SS *Capricorn* near the Sunshine Skyway Bridge in St. Petersburg, Florida. As the tanker's massive anchor became embedded in *Blackthorn*, the cutter twisted and sank within 10 minutes, taking the lives of 23 of the *Blackthorn*'s 50 crew members.

While the chief mission of most buoy tenders is to serve as aids to navigation, the *Blackthorn* had also been used as an icebreaker on the Great Lakes. The vessel also had a history of supporting various rescue and salvage operations.

A granite memorial commemorating this incident—the largest peacetime loss of life for the Coast Guard—was dedicated on January 28, 1981. Located at the north side of the Sunshine Skyway Bridge in St. Petersburg, an annual ceremony featuring an honor guard and bagpipes commemorating the crew serves as a solemn reminder of the dangers facing Coast Guard crews.

CUBAN RESCUE

In April 1980, Cuban president Fidel Castro announced that the country's Port Mariel was now open and Cubans were free to travel from the country. Excited citizens began boarding vessels—sometimes ignoring safety—to leave the country and come to the United States. After Castro's announcement, nearly 125,000 Cubans migrated to the United States. More than 1,000 Coast Guard vessels responded, assisted by boats and sailors from the U.S. Navy. Most of the "Marielitos," as these refugees came to be called, landed in Miami. Some were instead sent to centers in Indiantown Gap, Pennsylvania; Fort McCoy, Wisconsin; and Fort Chaffee, Arkansas, for immigration processing.

The rescue operation nearly overwhelmed Coast Guard crews, who worked to protect the lives of those who were leaving Cuba in boats sometimes piloted by inexperienced sailors. By May, two navy amphibious warfare ships arrived to help the Coast Guard patrol the seas. The services worked together to search for capsized vessels and struggling swimmers. Each day, the Coast Guard conducted air patrols in the waters closest to Key West, Florida, and Cuba, aided by the U.S. Navy.

The overloaded boats—few of which were stocked with appropriate safety gear—raised major concerns about this mass migration. In May 1980, Admiral John B. Hayes held a news conference to discuss the boats coming from Cuba and the safety concerns the Coast Guard had for Cubans. Hayes cited previous incidents in which unregulated boats were

After Fidel Castro allowed Cubans to leave the country from Mariel Harbor, the Coast Guard reacted quickly to protect many inexperienced sailors.

overloaded with people with insufficient safety gear. Out of concern that a maritime tragedy could occur, he appealed to the Cuban government in the interest of safety of life at sea.

After Hayes's press conference, the Coast Guard and other agencies came up with a strategy for responding to the humanitarian and legal issues raised by the increase of boats on American shores. Originally deployed to perform search-and-rescue operations, the Coast Guard and navy sailors would now be part of a law enforcement mission. Using radio broadcasts, the Coast Guard announced it was illegal to sail in an unauthorized vessel and pick up people. Vessels with obvious and dangerous safety violations were escorted into port until the violations were addressed. Commercial vessels carrying large numbers of immigrants without entry visas were detained. Reports from Port Mariel sounded chaotic. Refugees said the harbor had turned into a police state. Under threat of violence, the vessel *Atlantis* was ordered to transport 354 refugees with only 80 lifejackets aboard. In response, the Coast Guard cutter *Dallas* responded to escort the fishing vessel to Key West. For their actions during this time, the Coast Guard and navy received special recognition from President Jimmy Carter.

In June 1980, President Carter also allowed the Coast Guard commandant to call his reserve units into active duty for a maximum of six weeks. Coast Guard reservists, auxiliarists, and active-duty sailors worked together in perfect unison to carry out their mission and protect the lives of Cuban refugees. By the end of the month, 600 reserve sailors had joined the operation. Overall, the Mariel Boatlift—as this time was eventually named—highlighted the strengths of the historic Coast Guard while laying the foundation for the service's future. The Coast Guard's unique combination of lifesaving and military operations during this time helped save the lives of thousands of refugees and immigrants—all of whom were boaters in distress.

CHAPTER 4

MISSIONS IN THE MODERN WORLD

With fewer than 50,000 active-duty members, the Coast Guard is the smallest of the U.S. armed service branches. However, the service has always been renowned for its ability to quickly react to any dangerous situation and rapidly provide aid. In the 21st century, the Coast Guard has continued to prove its value by protecting some of the United States' biggest ports in Boston, Massachusetts, Washington, D.C., and New York City. This was especially true after the September 11, 2001, terrorist attacks, when Coast Guard units were called up for immediate duty to protect the nation's ports and harbors.

MARITIME SUPPORT FOR A DESERT CONFLICT

The valuable work Coast Guard crews perform has received more focused attention since the terrorist attacks on September 11, 2001. As part of the nation's response to these attacks, the entire Coast Guard displayed admirable adaptability and flexibility. That is nothing new for a military organization that has changed several times during more than two centuries of history. During Operation Iraqi Freedom, Coast Guard units provided port security for all U.S. military operations. More than 68 percent of its reserve force participated in these missions. In late 2002, a small fleet of Coast Guard vessels—cutters, patrol boats, a buoy tender, and their crews and support teams—were deployed to the Middle East and participated in maritime interception operations, coastal patrols, mine clearance, and search-and-rescue missions. They also maintained security for the Iraqi oil terminals in the North Arabian Gulf.

The buoy tender *Walnut* was part of many important missions while deployed to the region, including a search-and-rescue operation for the crews of two British Royal Navy helicopters that collided and setting navigational buoys to open waterways. In addition, the commanding officers from the patrol boats *Adak*, *Aquidneck*, *Baranof*, and *Wrangell* were awarded Bronze Stars for serving on the front defensive lines for coalition naval forces during the amphibious assault on Iraq's Al Faw Peninsula and for clearing mines within Iraqi territorial waters.

Though the newly announced "war on terror" was based on battles in the desert, Coast Guardsmen and women were also part of the fighting. In April 2004, Coast Guard Petty Officer Third Class Nathan Bruckenthal prepared to board a vessel off the coast of Iraq as part of a crew of navy sailors and one other Coast Guardsman. It was a trap. As they approached the vessel, it exploded. The attack killed Bruckenthal and two navy sailors. Bruckenthal's legacy inspires other brave men and women of the Coast Guard, all of whom accept the risk of serving in the U.S. armed forces. Even as the Coast Guard faces shifting missions, its members train constantly to carry on the proud tradition of maritime skills, including law enforcement and coastal protection.

PROTECTING THE SEAS

In modern times, Coast Guard teams continue to learn about and train on how to contain oil spills to protect ocean wildlife and coastal wetlands. Through the use of cutting-edge technical instruments and researchers at the Coast Guard's renowned research and design facility in Connecticut, personnel can detect the origin of a spill just as it is possible to link a footprint to a shoe. Careful study and gathering of evidence help Coast Guard teams pinpoint the ship that spilled the oil, even once it has left the scene.

When not protecting the nation, the Coast Guard spends time researching and reacting to oil spills and other maritime disasters.

The Coast Guard also maintains a National Strike Team that can rapidly deploy to manage spills and other disasters. This team was on duty when the shuttle *Columbia* broke up over Texas and other states in January 2003. A similar unit, called the Gulf Strike Team, responded to Boca Raton, Florida, in October 2001, when anthrax—a deadly chemical—was detected in the AMI Building. Using reservist members with civilian job skills, the team from Mobile, Alabama, displayed world-class knowledge and abilities while collaborating with other environmental agencies.

GOING ON A RAID

During the conflicts in Afghanistan and Iraq, Coast Guard members were asked to perform critical missions as part of the redeployment assistance and inspection detachment, or RAID. These teams were spread throughout Afghanistan and Iraq and were responsible for inspecting freight containers moving into, out of, and within the countries. The containers they investigated could hold anything, from food to ammunition. As Coast Guard inspectors look at containers, they are watchful for their structural safety, seaworthiness, and hazardous material labeling. The service has a long history of effectively inspecting containers, making the Coast Guard a natural choice for this assignment. At the peak of the conflict, RAID was examining nearly 300 containers per month, and RAID members traveled to remote areas of the country with land convoys, logging tens of thousands of miles per year. RAID service is hazardous duty, and many of the RAID members were exposed to mortar attacks and direct and indirect enemy gunfire.

ASSISTING THOSE IN NEED

The Coast Guard continues to train for and perform critical lifesaving search-and-rescue missions. The service has two centuries of training and tradition in this important field. Each year, the Coast Guard responds to tens of thousands of incidents and helps save thousands of lives.

The Coast Guard takes its lifesaving functions very seriously.

By law, the Coast Guard is required to respond to boaters in distress up to 20 nautical miles at sea. Updated and improving technology has dramatically improved the Coast Guard's ability to receive radio transmissions—even in poor weather and from outdated radios. The most important goal is a safe, swift, and successful rescue, and an accurate location of the vessel in need helps the Coast Guard accomplish these goals.

The Coast Guard is always designing and installing upgrades to its communication system. The service encourages boaters to use Emergency Position Indicating Radio Beacons (EPIRBs) attached to life vests in case a vessel capsizes. Boaters can also get free vessel safety checks from the Coast Guard Auxiliary. Similar to the reserve units from other military branches, the Auxiliary serves as the volunteer arm of the Coast Guard and has more than 30,000 members. Boating safety classes are offered online and in-person by the Coast Guard and its supporters. Education helps boaters prepare for emergency situations until the Coast Guard can arrive.

Because the Coast Guard patrols the entire stretch of U.S. coastline, it is prepared to handle many missions simultaneously. While scanning the shoreline and ports for national security threats, crews also pay close attention for signs of boaters in distress. From the earliest days of piracy on the high seas, the Coast Guard has developed powerful systems for detecting danger. These include random boat boardings that allow crews to gather information, partnerships

The Auxiliary is a strong volunteer support network for the Coast Guard.

developed with other agencies, and public awareness campaigns. The service also instructs boaters about safety equipment, such as life vests and flares. Visibility helps prevent accidents at sea and adds a measure of security to ports. Sometimes, divers and robots are used to inspect the underside of boats, bridges, and ports. Coast Guard Auxiliarists add a uniformed presence to docks and ports, and their heightened visibility allows for extended coastal protection and boater safety.

Though the Coast Guard must often enforce safe boating practices, environmental regulations, and laws—including writing tickets or arresting boaters—there is a true humanitarian component to the work it is asked to perform. Nowhere is that more evident than in the operations aimed at rescuing people lost at sea. The Mariel Boatlift in the 1980s was just one widely discussed Coast Guard search-and-rescue operation. Every day, the service deploys its members to potentially dangerous locations to help those who are calling for aid.

A FLEXIBLE SERVICE

In the early days of its existence, the Revenue Cutter Service was part of the Department of Commerce. It made good sense at the time, since its duties were primarily centered on trade and protecting the economic stability of a young nation. In 1967, President Lyndon Johnson transferred the Coast Guard into the Department of Transportation. However, it technically remained one of five military branches and would be moved under the leadership of the Department of the Navy in times of war. The seagoing service was still mainly interested in protecting commerce, and it continued to ensure the safety of marine transportation and the free flow of trade.

By the 21st century, expanded missions and evolving global situations brought the Coast Guard even more attention in the United States. Missions to protect homeland security were easily included as part of port security, law enforcement, marine environmental protection, and search-and-rescue missions—things with which the Coast Guard has always been comfortable.

It was not a huge surprise when, in 2003, the Coast Guard was moved into the newly created Department of Homeland Security. This agency was established by President George W. Bush to address future threats to the United States. Because the Coast Guard is used to having many duties, it emerged as a strong core for the agency because the service could respond so well and so rapidly to many new challenges.

POSITIONS AT SEA

It takes a team with diverse talents to run an organization like the Coast Guard. Because of the service's relatively small size, efficiency is its most defining characteristic. Behind the scenes, there are countless administrative support staff who keep the Coast Guard running. From lawyers preparing documents to officers ensuring that education benefits are understood, the Coast Guard makes sure that its crews are ready to serve at all times. Health specialists work at clinics, readying crews for critical missions in the United States and overseas.

Maintaining navigational aids, meal preparation, law enforcement, radio communications, aircraft repair, drug enforcement, and boat piloting are some of the varied jobs dedicated Coast Guard personnel pursue. The term "shipmate" is used to describe the culture of members of the service looking out for one another. That culture is especially attractive to the children of former Coast Guardsmen and women who want to continue the legacy their parents started.

WORKING PROTECTION

As a case in point for the Coast Guard's modern duties, look no further than the 2012 Republican National Convention (RNC). Though it seems unusual for the Coast Guard to be involved in a political convention, this 2012 event had some security concerns that the Coast Guard was uniquely qualified to address. Held at the Tampa Bay Times Forum next to Tampa's convention center, the 2012 RNC venue was surrounded by water. To reach the convention space, delegates would be crossing from any of 13 bridges from many hotels more than 20 miles (32.2 km) away. Given the high-profile nature of the event, any threat to the RNC could prove to be a national security risk. Preventing an attack was deemed to be a priority. The Coast Guard conducted painstaking planning to create a comprehensive waterside safety and security strategy. The convention's proximity to the Port of Tampa and its cruise ship terminals added additional challenges and safety precautions.

The Coast Guard's response to the RNC's potential vulnerabilities shows the flexibility and experience of its officers and sailors. Working with local and state organizations, the Coast Guard called for

The Coast Guard provided special protection for the 2012 RNC because of the unique security threats posed by its waterfront location.

an increase in patrols around the harbor. The combined forces also increased inspections of incoming commercial and recreational ships. On the night of the event, special security zones were established in the waters near the convention center. The Coast Guard also worked with civilian agencies, including groups in maritime industries, to spread awareness about the heightened security around the RNC. This multilevel approach to problem solving is one of the most important parts of the modern Coast Guard's success.

CHAPTER 5

WHAT IT MEANS TO SERVE

For many years, the United States relied on a draft to gather troops for the military. This meant that the U.S. armed forces were not all volunteers—some young men were forced to join because their names were selected as part of the draft. The United States went to an all-volunteer military in 1973, meaning that everyone who currently serves in the armed forces is there because they want to protect their country. Many young people feel this patriotic call, and the Coast Guard is an attractive option for those who wish for a life at sea.

ESTABLISHING ELIGIBILITY

Life in the military includes wearing a uniform, sticking to strict dress codes, and following regulations, customs, and traditions. The Coast Guard's lengthy history of honoring and respecting established traditions can be found in the service's motto: "Honor, Respect and Devotion to Duty." Both enlisted men and women and officers can be assigned to work in offices, on ships and aircraft, and at small-boat stations. Coast Guard stations can be found throughout the United States and its territories, although overseas assignments are also available.

Military life, even in the Coast Guard, is based on discipline and obedience to authority.

Before joining the Coast Guard, any potential member must meet certain standards. Requirements for applicants include:

- Being between 17 and 28 years of age
- Holding a high school diploma or GED
- Being a U.S. citizen or resident alien
- Being able to meet physical requirements
- Passing a vision and hearing exam
- Earning good scores on the Armed Forces Vocational Aptitude Battery (ASVAB) test

Once eligible, an applicant can speak with a recruiter either locally or online. Once accepted by the Coast Guard, recruits are sent to boot camp for two months at the Coast Guard Training Center in Cape May, New Jersey. Before training begins, recruits must sign a contract that describes the terms of their service in the Coast Guard. The contract provides the details of pay, rate and rank, G.I. Bill education benefits, military clothing allowance, and money for housing, food, and board.

As part of boot camp, recruits must complete intensive physical fitness training and classroom instruction. Included in this training are courses on first aid, weapons handling, sailing, shipboard firefighting, safety, survival in water, and nautical terminology.

EARNING RANK

Enlisted Coast Guardsmen and women are eligible for promotion after they complete on-the-job training and meet high qualifications. These requirements are stricter than the standards for entry into the Coast Guard, and they include professional military accomplishments and job-specific duties. Biannual evaluations can help enlisted Coast Guard members lay out paths for further career development. Once in the Coast Guard, there are several options for receiving a promotion. Competition for Officer Candidate School (OCS) is tough. Here are some of the requirements:

- Being between 21 and 35 years of age
- Meeting character standards for financial responsibility and moral judgment
- Being a U.S. citizen (born or naturalized)
- Having a bachelor's degree or higher
- Having a rank of E-5 or above
- Earning SAT scores of 1100 or higher or ASVAB scores of 109 or higher

LEARNING FROM THE BEST

Founded in 1876, the Coast Guard Academy is located in New London, Connecticut. Its motto represents the spirit of the service: "The sea yields to knowledge." For young people who want to

FOLLOWING A CREED

Each branch of the U.S. military follows its own set of philosophies and principles, making each unique. The Coast Guard is proud to stand behind a written set of ideals called the Creed of the United States Coast Guardsman, which was written by Vice Admiral Harry G. Hamlet, commandant of the service from 1932 to 1936.

- I am proud to be a United States Coast Guardsman.
- I revere that long line of expert seamen who by their devotion to duty and sacrifice of self have made it possible for me to be a member of a service honored and respected, in peace and in war, throughout the world.
- I never, by word or deed, will bring reproach upon the fair name of my service, nor permit others to do so unchallenged.
- I will cheerfully and willingly obey all lawful orders.
- I will always be on time to relieve, and shall endeavor to do more, rather than less, than my share.
- I will always be at my station, alert, and attending to my duties.
- I shall, so far as I am able, bring to my seniors solutions, not problems.
- I shall live joyously, but always with due regard for the rights and privileges of others.
- I shall endeavor to be a model citizen in the community in which I live.
- I shall sell life dearly to an enemy of my country, but give it freely to rescue those in peril.
- With God's help, I shall endeavor to be one of His noblest Works . . . A UNITED STATES COAST GUARDSMAN.

potentially become Coast Guard officers, the academy is the most prestigious path toward earning a commission. However, getting into the school is difficult. For those who do well in high school and put together a strong application, tuition, room, and board can be free. Students also receive uniforms and pay. There is one "catch": After graduation, a five-year service obligation is required. Getting into the Coast Guard Academy is slightly different from the other four military service academies. Students require a high grade-point average and good SAT scores, as opposed to a congressional appointment for admittance.

The U.S. Coast Guard Academy has been training the service's finest young officers since 1876.

There are thousands of applications annually for just 300 positions. Eligibility requirements include:

- Presenting strong grades and competitive SAT or ACT scores
- Being physically fit and having good athletic skills
- Being highly motivated and interested in leadership development

For students entering their senior year of high school, the Academy Introduction Mission program offers a five-day orientation program that is highly realistic. It allows the potential student to see what life in the school is like; the academy also gets to determine if the applicant has the skill, desire, and determination to succeed in such a program. It provides competition based in science, boating, and engineering principles.

Once they have earned their spot in the academy, cadets spend time sailing aboard the barque *Eagle*, America's tall ship and the Coast Guard Academy's training vessel. The academy is academically challenging, and leadership training gradually advances throughout the four-year degree program. The four-year curriculum includes marine engineering, naval architecture, marine and environmental science, government, and management. Cadets graduate with a bachelor of science degree and a commission in the United States Coast Guard.

OPTIONS FOR PART-TIMERS

On February 19, 1941, Congress passed the Coast Guard Reserve and Auxiliary Act. This new policy created a part-time force to support and augment the regular Coast Guard. Reservists serve two days a month and train an additional two weeks on active duty annually. Though they typically keep to these lighter schedules, reservists have been deployed on extended active duty to support hurricane and oil spill responses. Reservists have also been tasked with supporting the active-duty force in a variety of mission areas, such as port security and law enforcement at home and abroad. The Coast Guard

Taking a part-time position in the Coast Guard Reserve is an excellent way to get experience in the service while maintaining a civilian lifestyle.

is allowed to have nearly 10,000 reservists. The Reserve motto is "professionalism, patriotism and preparedness," a philosophy that reflects the varied missions reservists perform. Reservists provide skill and expertise in a wide variety of areas, including boat handling, law enforcement, marine environmental protection, marine safety, public affairs, and administrative work.

Because the Coast Guard's different units are asked to conduct many important missions, reservists have been called for active-duty missions more frequently. They have deployed in support of devastating hurricane response and recovery efforts, helped with advanced NASA shuttle operations, worked on emergency pollution responses, and supported an array of national and VIP special security events, such as the Super Bowl. From constant security patrols at ports during Operation Enduring Freedom in Afghanistan to the harbor and shoreside security patrols near the vulnerable ports, reservists play an important role in the Coast Guard.

Reservists are not the only part-time members of the Coast Guard. Another important division is called the Coast Guard Auxiliary, an all-volunteer arm of the Coast Guard. Auxiliarists provide education to civilian boaters who may not have a lot of experience. Founded in 1939, the Auxiliary is dedicated to supporting the Coast Guard through air and water patrols, teaching boating safety courses, and raising public awareness of boating issues. Recently, auxiliarists have been allowed to take on additional roles. Auxiliarists work similarly to volunteers in a hospital. They answer phones, teach non-specialist courses, fly their own aircraft, or pilot their own vessels as part of search-and-rescue operations. Their reliable, voluntary service makes these civilians an important—and welcome—part of the Coast Guard family.

COAST GUARD CAREERS

In the Coast Guard, the term "rate" is used to describe the type of job someone performs. Many Coast Guard careers have direct counterparts in the civilian world. This allows Guardsmen and women to easily transfer their skills to new jobs when they leave the service. As might be expected, most careers in the Coast Guard are related to boating. However, there are also many rates that offer support and other special roles. The following is a partial listing of rates and responsibilities:

- Aviation survival technician: Inspects, services, and repairs aircraft and provides safety training
- Boatswain's mate: Serves on all types of Coast Guard ships as a master of seamanship
- Damage controlman: Welds and cuts metal for repairs; fights fires; repairs plumbing, buildings, and ships; and helps

identify and decontaminate chemical and biological weapons

- Electrician's mate: Installs, maintains, and repairs electrical equipment on ships and ashore
- Food service specialist: Prepares food at stations and on ships
- Gunner's mate: Serves as specialist in small arms, including pistols, rifles, and machine guns
- Health services technician: Provides health care services for members of the Coast Guard
- Machinery technician: Operates and maintains all types of Coast Guard machinery
- Marine science technician: Investigates pollution events and oversees pollution cleanups, patrols harbors for safety and security, and boards foreign vessels to enforce pollution and navigation laws
- Storekeeper: Responsible for keeping a stock of clothing, parts, and other supplies, and distributes equipment to Guardsmen and women as appropriate.

One especially unique job in the Coast Guard is as a musician. Though musical instruments are not typically associated with military service, the United States Coast Guard Band has long been ranked among the best military bands in the world. Headquartered in New London, this band draws from graduates of the Coast Guard Academy. Members play music—both military-related and from other genres—at famous venues across the world. Though the Coast Guard is most often associated with sailing seas and inland waterways, there is truly a career path for anyone in the service.

The Coast Guard maintains its own group of elite musicians, who play a mixture of military marches and other pieces.

CHAPTER 6

AS DIVERSE AS THE NATION

Women and people of color have a long history of serving honorably in the Coast Guard. However, for much of the service's history, equality was not a focus. Things have changed in the modern world, and now the Coast Guard finds outstanding strength in its diverse members, who come from all types of backgrounds.

BLACK AMERICANS SERVING WITH HONOR

From the early days of the Revenue Cutter Service until 1843, enslaved people were forced to serve in the Coast Guard as stewards, cooks, and low-ranked sailors. In 1865, after the bloody Civil War, Black Americans were freed by the Thirteenth Amendment to the Constitution. Some newly freed Black Americans voluntarily joined the Revenue Cutter Service. In 1875, the Life-Saving Service employed a small number of Black Americans, who were stationed at lifesaving outposts across the eastern seaboard.

The only all-Black crew in the history of the Coast Guard operated Station 17 at Pea Island, North Carolina. While all members of this unit were former enslaved people, its leader—Captain Richard Etheridge—was a celebrated Civil War veteran. When an all-white crew refused to serve under his leadership, he appointed an all-Black crew. Over the years, Etheridge's crew saved men, women, and children in many notable and daring rescues. Etheridge specially prepared drills and training to hone the skills of his lifesaving crews. This unit became well known for rescues off the dangerous and rocky North Carolina Coast.

The crew was awarded the Gold Lifesaving Medal nearly a full century after its courageous rescue of all passengers aboard the *E.S. Newman*, which had run aground as a hurricane struck the Outer Banks of North Carolina. When Etheridge and his

Captain Etheridge led a group of free Black men to great success in the Coast Guard.

crew arrived on the scene, the conditions were so bad that they could not use their standard rescue equipment. By creatively tying lines around two Pea Island crew members, the lifesavers could alternate and make eight separate swimming trips out to the ship and rescue passengers in the pounding surf and dangerous conditions. One of Etheridge's men, Theodore Meekins—who had served for more than

40 years—eventually drowned during a particularly tough rescue.

In 1887, Captain Michael A. "Roaring" Healy became the only Black American to command a cutter before the official establishment of the Coast Guard. From 1887 to 1895, Healy served as commanding officer of the cutter *Bear*, catching illegal seal hunters, bringing medical supplies to Alaskans, preparing navigational charts, and documenting ice and weather reports. By the time of Healy's retirement, he had achieved the third-highest officer rank in the Revenue Cutter Service.

By the turn of the 21st century, major advances had been made in equality across the U.S. military. Vince Patton, a young native of Detroit, Michigan, was an Eagle Scout who aspired to serve at sea because his older brother served in the navy. Patton joined the Coast Guard and immediately set his sights on becoming the master chief petty officer of the Coast Guard, or MCPOCG—the Coast Guard's senior enlisted leader. Almost 30 years later, Patton achieved his goal when he was selected to serve as the first Black MCPOCG. His service ran from 1998 to 2002.

As MCPOCG, Master Chief Patton served as a senior adviser to the commandant of the Coast Guard and the secretaries of transportation and defense. He was responsible for speaking on issues affecting the tens of thousands of active-duty, reserve enlisted, and civilian personnel working for the Coast Guard.

Today, Black Guardsmen and women are a critical part of the efficient lifesaving and security force that they helped build.

PEOPLE OF COLOR: DISTINGUISHED SERVICE

Since 1877, Native Americans have also been proud members of the Coast Guard. Native Americans first comprised a lifesaving station crew at Neah Bay, Washington. Native Americans also served in the U.S. Lighthouse Service before the official creation of the U.S. Coast Guard. Through the 20th and 21st centuries, Native Americans did great work at lighthouses, including Point Arena, California, and Gay Head, Massachusetts.

During his service at Gay Head, Charles W. Vanderhoop was the only Native American principal lighthouse keeper. Petty Officer Joseph R. Toahty was a member of the Pawnee Nation. As a trained coxswain, Toahty participated in landing operations at Guadalcanal and Tulagi in the Pacific. Both men have been credited with important rescues.

Hispanic Americans primarily served effectively by achieving success in the Coast Guard as lighthouse keepers in the 1800s and early 1900s. The Revenue Cutter Service and the U.S. Life-Saving Service also welcomed Hispanic members. In 1920, Mess Attendant First Class Arthur Flores and Seaman John Gomez were both awarded the Silver Lifesaving

Though the U.S. military has an uneven history of diversity and inclusion, today's Coast Guard promotes equality for people of all races and genders.

Medal for heroism after they saved survivors of the schooner *Isaiah K. Stetson*, which sank off the coast of Massachusetts. Hispanic Americans continued their service through World War II and other conflicts in the 20th century.

Retired master chief petty officer Luis Diaz spent 22 years on active duty and 6 years as a civilian public affairs officer in Miami, Florida. Diaz was the first Puerto Rican to reach the rank of chief petty officer, senior chief petty officer, and master chief petty officer. A veteran who served in many important military operations—including Vietnam while in the navy—he also worked on the 1994 mass migration of Haitian and Cuban refugees and many hurricane recovery efforts, as well as operations related to cruise ships at sea.

Asian Americans have also been part of the lengthy history of Coast Guard service. Many Asian Guardsmen have served in the U.S. Lighthouse Service. Manuel Ferreira—a native of Maui—began his career as a lighthouse keeper with the Lighthouse Service in 1908. He eventually retired from the Coast Guard in 1946. Ferreira was in charge of seven lighthouses throughout Hawaii. During World War II, Florence Ebersole Smith Finch—a Filipino—became the only member of SPAR to receive the Pacific Campaign ribbon. As part of the overall war effort, Finch smuggled food into Manila's prison camps before she was captured by enemy forces. After being rescued by U.S. troops, she was one of only a handful of women to be awarded the U.S. Medal of Freedom.

Florence Finch is one of the most heroic Guardswomen in the history of the service.

Manuel Tubella Jr. was the first Filipino American aviator in the Coast Guard, and he was a reservist as well. Captain Kwang-Ping Hsu was a distinguished Coast Guard aviator who served for three decades with distinction.

In the 21st century, Asian Americans in the Coast Guard continue a rich tradition started more than a century ago in the U.S. Lighthouse Service.

CLIMBING THE RANKS

The first women to ever serve as second in command of a military service was Vivien S. Crea. She achieved the rank of vice commandant in the Coast Guard. Her resume includes a series of "firsts":

- First female air-station commander, and commander, Atlantic Area and Maritime Defense Zone
- First female presidential aide (serving under President Ronald Reagan)
- First woman to achieve flag officer status in the Coast Guard

Crea is one of only a few pilots to have flown the C-130 Hercules, the H-65 Dolphin helicopter, and the Gulfstream II jet. During her service, she earned four Legion of Merit awards, the Defense Superior Service Medal, and the Meritorious Service Medal.

COAST GUARD WOMEN

As early as the 1830s, women were serving as lighthouse keepers in the Lighthouse Service. In the mid-20th century, SPARs made numerous contributions to the war effort throughout World War II. Although the group was officially deactivated in 1947, many have noted that the U.S. Coast Guard Women's Volunteer Reserve—established in January 1950—rose to take its place.

In 1973, the Women's Reserve was shut down and women were given equal active-duty status in the Coast Guard. Two years later, some Guardswomen began to train as pilots. In 1976, the Coast Guard Academy admitted its first female students. Female soldiers in the U.S. military are now allowed to serve on the front lines in combat roles, but the Coast Guard had lifted barriers to women several decades ago, well before new equality policies were implemented in the 2010s.

The Coast Guard is a globally recognized effective military force, and much of its strength comes from its diversity. Women and people of color have consistently provided their talents and experience to the Coast Guard, whether they serve as active-duty members or reservists. These brave Guardsmen and women make use of cutting-edge technology to carry out their missions on the water and in the air.

CHAPTER 7

VESSELS OF THE COAST GUARD

The Coast Guard relies on its many different vessels—whether at sea or in the air—to get members where they need to be, fast. Over the years, wooden ships have gone by the wayside in favor of technologically advanced metal-hulled vessels that can do incredible things. Just as the Coast Guard takes on a variety of missions—from lifesaving to environmental protection to military actions—its vessels come in a variety of shapes and sizes.

CATEGORIZING BOATS

As a mainly seafaring service, the Coast Guard has a variety of boats and ships in its arsenal. For the most part, they can be broken into two main categories: cutters and small boats. A cutter is any Coast Guard vessel 65 feet (19.8 m) in length or greater with adequate space for a crew to live on board. All vessels under 65 feet in length are classified as small boats, typically operating near shorelines and on inland waterways.

The Coast Guard's fleet has come a long way since the days of Alexander Hamilton. Modern cutters are sleek, high-tech vessels.

CUTTERS

The 378-foot (115 m) high endurance cutter (WHEC) class includes the largest cutters—not including icebreakers—ever built for the Coast Guard. WHEC vessels run on diesel engines and gas turbines, and they have propellers whose pitch can be manually controlled. They are equipped with helicopter flight decks, retractable hangars, and the facilities to support and house a full helicopter crew. Cutters in this category were introduced to the Coast Guard inventory in the 1960s. Highly versatile and capable of performing a variety of missions, WHEC vessels can be found operating all across the world's oceans.

ICEBREAKERS

When the RMS *Titanic* collided with an iceberg in 1912, more than 1,500 lives were lost at sea. Though it took a tragic loss of life, the public was now extremely aware of how hazardous ice in the ocean can be. Following the *Titanic* disaster, the U.S. Navy assigned two ships for patrol. However, the military soon ran short on personnel to crew these vessels. In 1914, when the Safety of Life at Sea Treaty was signed by the world's most powerful maritime powers, the Coast Guard—a natural leader because of its history of maintaining the safe flow of commerce—was given responsibility for ice patrol from the Chesapeake Bay to Maine. On the Great Lakes, where the navigable waterways are ordinarily filled with cargo ships, icebreaking became a priority to keep these important shipping channels open.

The polar class icebreakers are among the largest U.S. Coast Guard cutters. Each is 399 feet (122 m) long. These large, powerful vessels have been specifically designed for open-water icebreaking. They feature reinforced hulls, special icebreaking bows, and technology packages that make it much easier to consistently and safely break up ice. The *Polar Sea* and *Polar Star* were built in the 1970s. They continue to serve science and research teams in the Arctic and Antarctic areas, and they are also used to provide supplies to isolated stations. In the polar regions, heavy icebreakers have historically been the only surface ships capable of creating a safe passageway for resupplying scientific and military stations. The polar class ships have also been quick to respond to oil spills and search-and-rescue cases when necessary. These ships have helped expand human understanding of heavy ice and its impact on maritime navigation. The International Ice Patrol has used aircraft to locate the boundaries of ice fields, thus saving lives and money for international shipping companies.

TRAINING VESSELS

One of the Coast Guard's most iconic vessels is the *Eagle*, a three-masted ship called a barque. The *Eagle* is 295 feet (90 m) long and is based at the Coast Guard Academy in New London. This traditional ship serves as a way to teach cadets the fundamentals of sailing, while also providing outreach to the general public. It is one of just five such training barques in the world.

The *Eagle*'s patriotic name predates the official establishment of the United States Coast Guard. The first *Eagle* was commissioned in 1792, just two years after the founding of the Revenue Marine.

Today, the *Eagle* can serve about 175 cadets and instructors from the U.S. Coast Guard Academy at a time. Cadets are taught traditional seamanship principles on its decks.

On the wooden decks and rugged rigging of the *Eagle*, Coast Guard cadets are first confronted with sea challenges. From this experience, they develop a healthy respect for the wind, waves, and weather they will likely face while serving in the Coast Guard on the high seas. Each drill and exercise conducted on the *Eagle* is designed to test the limits of trainees' endurance. They learn to conquer fears they may have. The training that cadets receive on this sailing vessel prepares them for their Coast Guard careers. On the *Eagle*, Cadets have a chance to apply the navigation and engineering training they have received in classes at the academy. As upper-class cadets, they serve in junior-officer leadership roles. As under-class cadets, they act as the regular crew of the *Eagle*. Students watch the helm and steer the vessel using the giant brass and wood wheels. This allows them to experiment with Coast Guard duties from all perspectives. Teamwork is extremely important.

More than 200 lines of the *Eagle*'s rigging must be coordinated during a major ship maneuver, so cadets learn the name and function of each line while working in the rigging—working well above the decks and often while the ship is in motion. The steel hull of the *Eagle* is almost half an inch thick, but it moves easily through water. It can reach a top speed of 17 knots. At the Coast Guard Academy, the *Eagle* berths on the Thames River in Connecticut. About 1,000 cadets a year sail aboard the *Eagle*.

The *Eagle* is one of the Coast Guard's oldest and most iconic ships.

BUOY TENDERS

The 175-foot (53 m) Keeper class coastal buoy tenders represent cutting-edge advances in buoy tending technology. All of the ships in this class are named after historical lighthouse keepers. Keeper class vessels are the first Coast Guard cutters to have special propulsion units instead of the standard propeller and rudder. Unlike most vessels, these ships can rotate 360 degrees in the water. Combined with a thruster located in the bow, these unique propulsion units allow the Keeper class cutters to maneuver in the water like never before. This is important, because these vessels are used to check buoys, which are devices that help show ships safe passages through coastal waters. If the buoys are in the wrong place, a ship could hit a reef, drag across the ocean floor, or collide with another obstruction, possibly causing damage and endangering the lives of those on board.

The coastal buoy tenders' state-of-the-art electronics and navigation systems use a differential Global Positioning System (GPS). As a result, these cutters are able to maneuver and position buoys more accurately and efficiently—while requiring fewer Coast Guardsmen and women to put themselves at risk to crew them.

The Coast Guard's buoy tenders are unique ships that can service the needs of the nation's series of buoys, which are important navigational tools.

WHERE IN THE WORLD

Many different technologies have played a part in the Coast Guard's rise to global effectiveness, but among the most important is GPS. This system is a satellite-based navigation network that was developed and is operated by the U.S. Department of Defense. Modern GPS communications allow land-based, seafaring, and airborne users to determine their three-dimensional position, velocity, and time 24 hours a day, in all weather, anywhere in the world—with precision and accuracy. Though it was originally created to assist the Coast Guard and other branches of the U.S. military, GPS has also changed the way people navigate around the world.

Ocean navigation has always been a great challenge, but modern technology, including GPS, makes it eeasier than ever before.

PATROL BOATS

Island class 110-foot (33.5 m) patrol boats are similar to a type of British patrol boat. All Coast Guard boats in the Island class are named after U.S. islands. With the ability to go long distances, these boats replaced the older 95-foot (29 m) Cape class patrol boats. These cutters feature advanced electronics and navigation equipment to assist on long voyages.

SMALL BOATS

Small boats can typically be found operating near shorelines and on inland waterways. These vessels are smaller than cutters, ranging in size from 12 to 64 feet (3.7 to 19.5 m) in length. They include motor lifeboats, deployable pursuit boats, and rigid hull inflatable boats. As a broad category, the Coast Guard's small boats are chosen for their flexibility and because they can be easier to sail through shallower waters.

GUARDING THE SKIES

In addition to its maritime vessels, the Coast Guard employs hundreds of aircraft. Planes and helicopters are most commonly used for search-and-rescue missions, but they are also deployed for law enforcement, environmental response, and ice operations. Coast Guard airplanes are based at air stations, while Coast Guard helicopters operate from flight deck–equipped cutters, air stations, and air facilities located all over the world.

The Coast Guard makes use of many high-tech flying machines, including the HC-130 Hercules, a tactical military transport aircraft. Hercules planes feature integrated digital controls with heads-up displays that require minimal crews while maintaining high performance. The aircraft is used for all of the Coast Guard's primary mission areas: long-range search-and-rescue operations, law enforcement missions, airlifts, and homeland security.

The United States Coast Guard is equipped with more than 40 medium-range Sikorsky MH-60 Jayhawk helicopters. The Jayhawk's cutting-edge technology package includes advanced radar, radio, and navigational equipment. This technology enables the helicopter to carry out search-and-rescue, law enforcement, military readiness, and marine environmental protection missions.

Helicopters have become some of the Coast Guard's most effective aircraft because of their speed and versatility. One of the most common Coast Guard aircraft is the HH-65A Dolphin, a short-range helicopter that is commonly stationed onshore. However, because Dolphins are so light, they can also be transported on cutters for certain missions. Dolphins are especially useful for search-and-rescue and law enforcement operations, but they are also deployed to respond to pollution emergencies and to support other military operations.

The versatile and powerful HC-130 Hercules has been used by the Coast Guard since 1959.

CHAPTER 8

A BRIGHTER FUTURE ON THE COAST

For most of its history, the U.S. Coast Guard has been asked to do a little bit of everything. Though it is most well known for its lifesaving missions close to home, the service has frequently been involved in law enforcement operations and military actions across the world. The future is based on evolving advanced technology, and that means that the Coast Guard will increasingly need the assistance of new recruits who are passionate about serving their country with computer and robotics skills.

DESIGNED FOR THE FUTURE

For centuries, the men and women of the Coast Guard have worked hard to prevent drug smugglers and other criminals from reaching U.S. shores. Law enforcement, coastal border protection, the safe flow of commerce, and lifesaving missions all make up the Coast Guard's mission as a world-renowned protector of the nation's waterways and ports. Search-and-rescue crews are always on the lookout for threats to homeland security. Using advanced technology, including underwater robots, voiceless vessel transmissions, and advanced aircraft that can sense oil that is floating on water, the modern Coast Guard is a skilled and flexible force.

Because the Coast Guard operates on so many fronts, it must always balance the country's evolving security needs with its need to protect the marine environment and protect lives at sea. This flexibility and adaptability have been the defining features of the service, with foundations in the ever-changing needs of the United States and the international community. Though the Coast Guard is best known for its work along the nation's 95,000 miles (153,000 m) of coastline, the service also operates on navigable rivers and waterways and maintains safety within 360 primary ports. A rich maritime military tradition coupled with expertise in rescue, security, and law enforcement places greater importance on Coast Guard work than ever before. The Coast Guard enforces U.S. laws, international treaties, and maritime transportation laws while also providing security at ports, waterways, and shore facilities. Because of this, it is the lead agency for U.S. homeland defense. The Coast Guard also supervises and conducts icebreaking missions and protects the marine environment by enforcing fishery regulations. Coast Guard vessels are even used for transporting scientists to the North and South Poles.

Most of the changes to the Coast Guard over the last half-century have been related to the development and implementation of new technology. New missions and advanced operations call for new scientific advancements. Command and control systems allow the military to communicate with, track, and direct units from remote locations. Rescue 21 is a cutting-edge system that uses digital position tracking and allows the Coast Guard to talk directly to other first responders during emergencies. This command and control system helps the Coast Guard accurately relay the locations of boaters in trouble while also allowing it to track its own boats.

As potential threats continue to become more complex, the Coast Guard will become more important than ever for its expertise in search-and-rescue missions as well as law enforcement protection of ports and other commercial interests. Combating terrorism, ensuring port and cargo safety, and battling drug smugglers, polluters, and illegal immigrants will all continue to pose challenges in a changing world. For a young person who hears the call to the

The Coast Guard, like all modern military branches, relies on cutting-edge technology to complete its increasingly complex and important missions.

sea and wants to protect boaters in danger, a career in the Coast Guard can be an exciting opportunity.

THE GLORY OF THE COAST GUARD

Each branch of the U.S. armed forces has its own motto that sums up the mission and history of the service. The Coast Guard is no exception. Its motto—*Semper Paratus*—comes from the Latin for "always ready." Though most Coast Guard members are not called on to serve on global battlefields like other soldiers, they work just as hard as their more military counterparts. The Semper Paratus motto reflects the variety of missions the service is sent on, as well as the ability of Guardsmen and women to rapidly spring into action. The official Coast Guard march is titled "*Semper Paratus*," and it has its origins in the early 20th century. Originally written by Captain Francis von Boskerck, the song has been updated several times over the past century. The first verse and chorus are a strong summary of the Coast Guard's embodiment of the philosophy of always being prepared:

From Aztec shore to Arctic zone,
To Europe and Far East,
The Flag is carried by our ships,
In times of war and peace;
And never have we struck it yet,
In spite of foemen's might,
Who cheered our crews and cheered again,

For showing how to fight.
We're always ready for the call,
We place our trust in Thee.
Through surf and storm and howling gale,
High shall our purpose be.
"*Semper paratus*" is our guide,
Our fame, our glory too.
To fight to save, or fight to die,
Aye! Coast Guard we are for you!

GLOSSARY

amphibious Able to be used on both land and sea.

barque A three-masted sailing vessel.

bow The front, or pointy end, of a boat.

chart Map.

coxswain Enlisted person in charge of a boat.

cutter A vessel that is 65 feet (19.8 m) or longer with accommodations for the crew.

deck Nautical term for floor.

flare Safety device that can be lit so you can be seen, if in trouble.

helm The wheel or tiller that controls the rudder.

hull The main shell of a vessel.

knot The unit used to measure speed at sea.

mess A group that lives or works together on a ship (e.g., Chief Petty Officer's mess). It also refers to the meal itself or food in general or the area where food is eaten ("I'll meet you on the mess deck").

petty officer Enlisted person who is specially trained and rated.

reconnaissance A military action involving information gathering about an enemy.

rudder A board-shaped piece attached to the back of a ship or boat for steering and maneuvering.

sampan A flat-bottomed boat used in eastern Asia and usually propelled by two short oars.

schooner Sailing vessel with two or more masts.

smuggle Transporting goods secretly and illegally.

tariff A tax on goods that are coming into or leaving a country.

torpedo A special weapon fired underwater to destroy a ship.

FOR MORE INFORMATION

Go Coast Guard

Website: www.gocoastguard.com
Facebook and Instagram: @GoCoastGuard

This official recruiting website for the U.S. Coast Guard has a database of information about what it takes to join the branch and a direct link to apply.

Military.com: Coast Guard

133 Boston Post Road
Weston, MA 02493
Website: www.military.com/coast-guard
Facebook, Instagram, and Twitter:
@Militarydotcom

This website provides information on the history, current events, and career data for every branch of the U.S. service, including the Coast Guard.

United States Coast Guard

2703 Martin Luther King Jr. Avenue SE
Washington, DC 20020
Website: www.uscg.mil
Facebook: @UScoastguard
Instagram and Twitter: @USCG

This is the official hub for all Coast Guard information, including articles on breaking news and further reading about the divisions of the service.

The United States Coast Guard Academy

31 Mohegan Avenue
New London, CT 06320
Website: www.uscga.edu
Facebook: @CoastGuardAcademy
Instagram: @USCG_Academy
Twitter: @USCGAcademy

The U.S. Coast Guard Academy is the most prestigious college for those who want to work in the Coast Guard, and the official website has further information on the school and how to apply.

United States Coast Guard Auxiliary

9449 Watson Industrial Park
St. Louis, MO 63126
Website: cgaux.org

The official website of the Coast Guard Auxiliary provides information on the functions of this important branch of the service.

FOR FURTHER READING

Abdo, Kenny. *United States Coast Guard*. Minneapolis, MN: Abdo Zoom, 2019.

Baxter, Roberta. *Work in the Military*. San Diego, CA: BrightPoint Press, 2020.

Best, B. J. *Coast Guard Boats*. New York, NY: Cavendish Square, 2018.

Billings, Tanner. *The U.S. Coast Guard*. New York, NY: Rosen Publishing, 2022.

London, Martha. *U.S. Coast Guard Equipment and Vehicles*. Mendota Heights, MN: Kids Core, 2022.

McCarthy, Cecilia Pinto. *Life in the U.S. Coast Guard*. San Diego, CA: BrightPoint Press, 2021.

Mitchell, P. P. *Join the Coast Guard*. New York, NY: Gareth Stevens Publishing, 2018.

Orr, Tamra B. *Hurricane Katrina and America's Response*. Ann Arbor, MI: Cherry Lake Publishing, 2017.

Salter, Krewasky A. *The Story of Black Military Officers, 1861–1948*. New York, NY: Routledge, 2014.

Tougias, Mike. *Into the Blizzard: Heroism at Sea During the Great Blizzard of 1978*. New York, NY: Henry Holt, 2019.

Tougias, Mike. *A Storm Too Soon: A Remarkable True Survival Story in 80-Foot Seas*. New York, NY: Square Fish, 2017.

United States Coast Guard. *Learn About the United States Coast Guard*. Washington, DC: U.S. Coast Guard Community Relations, 2015.

Waeschle, Amy. *Daring Flood Rescues*. North Mankato, MN: Capstone Press, 2018.

INDEX

Y

ABOUT THE AUTHOR

Jessie George is a semiprofessional triathlete who has competed all over the world. In addition to reading and running, her greatest passion is for her three dogs.

CREDITS

Cover U.S. Coast Guard photo by Petty Officer 3rd Class Ross Ruddell; series background ensuper/Shutterstock.com; p. 5 https://commons.wikimedia.org/wiki/File:John_Trumbull_-_Alexander_Hamilton_-_Google_Art_Project.jpg; pp. 6, 11, 24, 35, 68 courtesy U.S. Coast Guard; p. 9 https://commons.wikimedia.org/wiki/File:Seal_of_the_United_States_Lighthouse_Service.png; p. 14 https://en.wikipedia.org/wiki/File:IdaLewis.jpg; p. 16 https://commons.wikimedia.org/wiki/File:Bertholf_portrait_3.jpg; p. 20 https://commons.wikimedia.org/wiki/File:President_Woodrow_Wilson_(1913).jpg; p. 22 U.S. Coast Guard photo by Petty Officer 2nd Class Tara Molle; p. 26 Jon Bilous/Shutterstock.com; p. 31 https://commons.wikimedia.org/wiki/File:K-74761.jpg; p. 34 U.S. Coast Guard photo by Petty Officer 1st Class Christopher Evanson; p. 39 https://en.wikipedia.org/wiki/File:USCGC_Active_(WMEC_618)_Mariel_Boatlift_(7352293542).jpg; p. 45 U.S. Coast Guard photo by Petty Officer 3rd Class Jonathan Klingenberg; p. 47 U.S. Coast Guard photo by Aux. William Greer; p. 49 USCGAUX Photo by Joseph P. Cirone; p. 53 U.S. Coast Guard photo by Petty Officer 1st Class Crystalynn A. Kneen; p. 55 U.S. Coast Guard photo by Petty Officer 3rd Class Amanda Levasseur; p. 59 USCG photo by David M. Santos PA1; p. 61 U.S. Coast Guard photo by Petty Officer 2nd Class Patrick Kelley; p. 65 U.S. Coast Guard photo by Petty Officer 2nd Class Richard Brahm; p. 71 U.S. Coast Guard photo by Petty Officer 3rd Class Anthony Pappaly; p. 73 U.S. Coast Guard photo by Senior Chief Petty Officer Alan Haraf; p. 77 Jon Bilous/Shutterstock.com; p. 81 Africadventures/Shutterstock.com; p. 83 U.S. Coast Guard photo by PA3 Annie R. Berlin; p. 84 U.S. Coast Guard photo by Petty Officer 3rd Class Amanda Norcross; p. 87 U.S. Coast Guard photo by Don Kluting; p. 91 U.S. Coast Guard photo by Chief Petty Officer Sara Muir/Released.

Designer: Michael Flynn; Editor: Siyavush Saidian